Monkey Grass

Poems for Those Who Are
Not All That Fond of Poetry

J.R. Dunworth

PublishAmerica
Baltimore

© 2006 by J.R. Dunworth.
All rights reserved. No part of this book may be reproduced, stored in a retrieval system or transmitted in any form or by any means without the prior written permission of the publishers, except by a reviewer who may quote brief passages in a review to be printed in a newspaper, magazine or journal.

First printing

All characters appearing in this work are fictitious. Any resemblance to real persons, living or dead, is purely coincidental.

ISBN: 1-4241-2941-9
PUBLISHED BY PUBLISHAMERICA, LLLP
www.publishamerica.com
Baltimore

Printed in the United States of America

Tastes Vary

Should this book for you provide
No great pleasure in its perusing,
Set it free upon the tide;
Surely someone'll find it amusing.

Table of Contents

LIFE STAGES

LAMENT 15
TIME PASSES WITH A CREAK AND A WHINE 16
ADVICE TO POTENTIAL RETIREES 17
MAKING GROWING PAINS PAINLESS 18
EVERY DAY IN EVERY WAY I'M GETTING
    BETTER AND BETTER 19
NOT ALL PROBLEMS HAVE SOLUTIONS 21
SEASONAL ADVENTURES 22

WINTER

OH, TO BE TEN AGAIN 25
HOT SOUP IS WINTER'S ANTIDOTE 26
IF YOU WANT TO GO TO HEAVEN
    DIE IN THE DEPTHS OF WINTER 27
WAITING FOR SPRING 28

SPRING

IT'S MARCH AGAIN! 31
PRAY FOR RAIN 32
THERE'S SOMETHING IN THE AIR 33
LATE SPRING 34

SUMMER

AN ANNUAL TRIBAL GATHERING 37
A SEASON FOR ALL MEN 38
THERE IS COMFORT IN A GOOD EXCUSE 39
MISSISSIPPI MOONLIGHT 40
SUMMERS LOST 41
THE DROUGHT HAS ENDED 42
SUMMER'S DRIPPING DECADENCE 43
ARE YOU SURE IT'S SEPTEMBER? 44
LABOR DAY BLUES 45

CULTURE

BECOMING AMERICAN: GENERATION I 49
BECOMING AMERICAN: GENERATION II 50
BECOMING AMERICAN: GENERATION III 51
WE'VE CHANGED 52
REDEFINING THE TEN SUGGESTIONS 53
THE RELATIVE WEIGHT OF VIRTUES AND VICES 54
PEOPLE WATCHING AT THE MALL 55
ON THE ROAD TO THE BALKAN STATES OF
    AMERICA 56
YOU CANNOT DEFAME THE DEAD 57

SPECIAL DAYS

A DAY TO REMEMBER 61
HAPPY DAY, VALENTINE! 62
THE FABULOUS FIRST 63
IT'S YOUR DAY 64
A NIGHT OF FRIGHT 65
CHILDREN AWAKENING TERRIFIED ON
   A COLD DECEMBER NIGHT 66
AN AMERICAN CHRISTMAS 67
A VERY MERRY YEAR-END FESTIVITIES
   CYCLE TO ALL 68

PETS

OH, TANNENBAUM! 71
A BEAUTIFUL STRAY CAME OUR WAY 72
A SUNNY MORNING
   ON THE LIVING ROOM CARPET 73
MONKEY GRASS REST STOP 74

POLITICS

THE WAY WE CHOOSE OUR LEADERS 77
EXERCISING THE VOTE 78
AMBITION 79

WAR AND PEACE

THE LEARNING EXPERIENCE 83
AND ON EARTH, PEACE TO MEN OF GOOD WILL ... 84
CELEBRATION 85
A JULY NIGHT ON FREEDOM'S TRAIL 86

THE SEA

WHY WE GO DOWN TO THE SEA IN SHIPS 89
STEAMING INTO THE WIND 90
THE SHALLOWS 91

THIS AND THAT

WE MUST ALL HUMOR ONE ANOTHER 95
HI, I'M FROM THE GOV'MENT AND I'M HERE
    TO HELP 96
ODE TO THE FALLEN 97
STARTING OVER 98
THE LILT OF IRISH MUSIC 99
A SLIGHTLY HEAVIER OUNCE OF PREVENTION 100
IT AIN'T NECESSARILY SO! 101
LIVING IN INTERESTING TIMES 102
THE ANATOMY OF HAIKU 103
THE LANGUAGE LIVES, BUT IT'S AILING 104

BIRTHDAYS

FOR MY FRESHEST GRANDCHILD	107
ONE YEAR OLD	108
TWO YEARS OLD	109
THREE YEARS OLD	110
FOUR YEARS OLD	111
FIVE YEARS OLD	112
SIX YEARS OLD	113
SEVEN YEARS OLD	114
EIGHT YEARS OLD	115
NINE YEARS OLD	116
TEN YEARS OLD	117
ELEVEN YEARS OLD	118
TWELVE YEARS OLD	119
THIRTEEN YEARS OLD	120

FOREWORD

Most of these poems were written for the *Memphis Mensa Newsletter*. "Summer's Dripping Decadence," which appeared in the August 2004 issue, was a last-minute substitution for a somewhat more controversial poem.

"Not All Problems Have Solutions" is not about what Spanish speakers refer to as a *viejo verde*. It was written on my first trip to sea after a 30-year hiatus. In 2003, at age 67, I took a berth as second mate in a containership. The last time I had sailed second mate I was in my twenties.

"Happy Day, Valentine!" and "It's Your Day" were written for my wife, Sofia, and are offered here with her permission. The impetus for "...And On Earth Peace..." was provided by the war in Afghanistan. "The Learning Experience" was written after Hurricane Katrina showed us we might need a bit more drill in the area of Homeland Security. "Steaming into the Wind" was written on 25 July 1970 en route from Manila to Yokohama in the SS *President Wilson*. We had been sailing for several days into a 30 to 35 kt relative wind from dead ahead. "The Shallows" is another 1970 poem. "Ode to the Fallen" was written on the occasion of the death of President Reagan.

The Birthday poems were written for grandchildren. There are seventeen of them and, in order of appearance, they are: Octavia, Ricardo, Sofía, Benjamin, John, Michelle, Nicole, Michaela, Kyle, Karina, Jacqueline, S. Elizabeth, Miguel, Lucas, Mariana, Ian, and Adrienne.

JRD

LIFE STAGES

LAMENT

I have a little belly
That hangs right o'er my belt;
Unless I lose that jelly,
I never will be svelte.

TIME PASSES WITH A CREAK AND A WHINE

After a certain point birthdays begin to lose their charm.
As life hurtles down its track,
Aches in muscle and joint tend to raise a certain alarm.
I passed that point some while back.

How old am I? One more six and I'll be marked by the Beast.
If there is a bright side to this fix,
It's just that I will most surely be out of here, at least,
Before I can get that third six.

ADVICE TO POTENTIAL RETIREES
(Annoying, but Effective)

We've all heard the stories about the guy
Who, healthy as a horse, worked forty years;
Retired, and before a year had gone by
Had produced a widow producing tears.

It seems he'd felt lost without his job.
With beer in hand he'd sat and watched the tube.
"There's nothing to do," whined this nabob
'Til he froze up beyond help of a lube.

If you're looking for activities
To keep you limber, warmish, and vital,
Rely on ancient amenities.
Old cars and houses won't leave you idle.

This week's project is leak repair, or
Roofing materials I'm learning about,
And hunting a radiator for
A '75 International Scout.

Annoying? You're right.
But effective? Quite!

MAKING GROWING PAINS PAINLESS

I have a little belly
That hangs right over my belt.
It jiggles just like jelly,
And flat refuses to melt.

I've tried getting rid of it
In ev'ry way that I know;
But just getting used to it
Might be the best way to go.

EVERY DAY IN EVERY WAY I'M GETTING BETTER AND BETTER

Every day, in every way, I'm getting smarter and smarter.
My teenage kids used to say I was dumb; dumb as dirt to be precise.
But now they can acknowledge kinship without feeling like a martyr.
The youngest is thirty-four, and all of them call to ask my advice.
Every day, in every way, I'm getting smarter and smarter.

Every day, in every way, I am getting much better groomed.
No more does dandruff whiten my day with millions of fluttering flakes.
Since my part widened to four inches and my follicles were entombed
I've had very little trouble with those little cranial snowflakes.
Every day, in every way, I am getting much better groomed.

Every day, in every way, I'm getting more and more moral.
When I was young, my morals were gray and my tastes ran to things sinful.
With the fact that I've not changed too much, there is very little quarrel.
But "pop" theology has decreed those sins passé by the bin full.
Every day, in every way, I'm getting more and more moral.

Every day, in every way, I'm getting stronger and stronger.
The list of my many feats of strength just continues to grow longer.

At twenty-five, I could not lift fifty dollars worth of groceries. Today, I can carry them in one hand. Fifty dollars, if you please! Every day, in every way, I'm getting stronger and stronger.

There's just no doubt about it. My eyes are brighter; my cheeks are redder.
Every day, in every way, I'm getting better and better.

NOT ALL PROBLEMS HAVE SOLUTIONS

When the frost is on the whiskers,
And the scalp is showing through;
When the face that's in your mirror doesn't seem to look like you;
When you start getting more respect than you really think
   you're due,
That's when something deep inside you
Just cries out to start anew.

And if you don't set your sight too high,
Reliving one's youth can be done.
But the first time around, bye the bye,
Is a helluva lot more fun.

SEASONAL ADVENTURES

The spring was great; a fine beginning;
An entrance gate; an early inning.

Then summertime for growth and learning;
It was a time for serious earning.

Autumn was best, when everything peaked;
The world possessed; and then something creaked.

We sense death's knell. Our time is thinning.
For fall has fell and winter's winning.

WINTER

OH, TO BE TEN AGAIN

Oh, to be ten again,
Or nine, or eight, or seven,
When snow is in the glen,
And sleds transport to heaven.
When skates glide effortlessly
And skaters race breathlessly
Across the hard frozen pond
To the creek mouth and beyond.

Sitting in a schoolroom was
Just pure agony because
Through the steamy window pane
Could be seen Jack Frost's domain—
The essence of life's leaven,
Frozen ponds and snowmen.
My idea of heaven.
Oh, to be ten again!

HOT SOUP IS WINTER'S ANTIDOTE

I like a little pepper in my soups.
Not very much, you understand,
Just enough to cause a Chef to say, "Oops."
In life and soups avoid the bland.

With my eyes tearing and my sinuses clearing,
I most happily slurp away.
With windows steaming and moonlit snow a-gleaming,
What better way to end a day!

If your life seems dull, with excitement in a lull,
When you just can't whoop, and your taste buds droop,
When you need a way to keep the winter at bay,
Then try a little pepper in your soup.

IF YOU WANT TO GO TO HEAVEN DIE IN THE DEPTHS OF WINTER

In the not so merry month of Febr'ary,
When the temp'rature drops down low,
All our fancies subside to the ord'nary
And the pace of our lives is slow.

Keeping warm tops our list of priorities;
Next is earning enough for heat.
No time's left to engage in debaucheries,
Pride, Prejudice, Pique, or Deceit.

March with its bipolar disorder, will splice
Itself into fancy-turning spring.
If, in the glories of which, we're not as nice,
Think of the comfort that it will bring.

WAITING FOR SPRING

In the very weary month of March,
When the wind blows blue from the Pole,
And your spine could really use some starch,
Just making it through is the goal.

SPRING

IT'S MARCH AGAIN!

St. Patrick's Day is a day I like.
Basketball, I can do without.
A warm spring day, and a trip by bike;
Wintry storms leave trees strewn about.

March is a month with some identity crises,
But spring will triumph leaving the House of Pisces.

PRAY FOR RAIN

If April showers bring May flowers,
What happens if it doesn't rain?
If the month is dry will flowers die?
Will beauty wane and ugly gain?

THERE'S SOMETHING IN THE AIR

In the merry, merry month of May,
'Tis a pleasure just to greet each day.
Won't you come and walk along?
Aren't you going my way?

Won't you help me sing my song?
Can't you come out to play?
Hand in hand, we will stroll all the day,
In the very merry Month of May.

LATE SPRING

Summer's comin'; summer's comin'.
Nests a-fillin'; bees a-hummin';
Bakin' sun and kids a-runnin'
Summer fun an' hot rods gunnin';
Hurry hon' an' plan us somethin'.
Summer's comin'; summer's comin'.

SUMMER

AN ANNUAL TRIBAL GATHERING

No mere words can adequately describe
That now long past, but still remembered sensation:
Attending the gathering of the tribe
On the very first day of summer vacation.

A brilliant sun looks down from the clear June sky,
And the smell of clover is on the air.
Breakfasts gulped, screen doors banged, steps cleared on the fly,
Children explode through back doors ev'rywhere.

Soon the entire tribe is gathered again.
For its yearly June to September race.
Between the ages of seven and ten,
The world is indeed a wonderful place.

A SEASON FOR ALL MEN

I like the summertime
More'n any other time.

I liked it as an infant
'Cause dressing was more instant.

I liked it as a child,
A time for running wild.

And when an adolescent,
I found soft nights quite pleasant.

Even working's more fun
When gray cold turns to sun.

And when the gray is in your hair
Your bones feel good when weather's fair.

I like the summertime
More'n any other time.

THERE IS COMFORT IN A GOOD EXCUSE

Half of my summer has gone;
Half of my summer's work has not.

Lots of guilt tries piling on.
It's not my fault. It's just too hot.

MISSISSIPPI MOONLIGHT

Summer nights in Mississippi
Have got a feel that's all their own.
Whether farm or sleepy city,
The scents of grass, recently mown,
And honeysuckle fill the air.

Fireflies wink, and the lovebugs pair.
Darkness softened in silver tone,
Night zephyrs are taking pity
On good folks sun baked to the bone
Summer nights in Mississippi.

SUMMERS LOST
(You done us dirt, Mr. Carrier)

It's summer, and the air is syrupy thick
In a neighborhood nestled under ancient trees.
A porch Swing's soft creak, a hall clock's tick-tock-tick,
An ancient, slumbering hound's gentle snore and wheeze,
At the back of the house a window fan clicks
Its nearly successful attempt to stir a breeze.

It's summer. Children's voices are ev'rywhere,
Chasing balls in bright sunlight and fireflies at dusk.
Day's oppressive heat fades to night's soft, sweet air:
Blossoms' fragrances; new mown grass gives off its musk.

Young love holds hands; old love sits and swings and talks.
Dim, bug-swarmed street lights pierce the blackness here and there.
Moonrise finds people finishing ev'ning walks.
Cots appear and a porch becomes a moon drenched lair.
And so it was—yesterday; but not today.
Today, machinery keeps our summers at bay.

From air conditioned house to air conditioned car,
To air conditioned office, then back to the car;
An air conditioned theater or rest'rant finishes our day;
Then to our air conditioned storage to await another day.

We've lost something, but no one wants to return
To those good old days of fans and wrinkled suits.
It's for our youth, not discomfort that we yearn—
For slower life and connection with our roots.
I'm afraid we can't go back, and I expect it will just get worse
As we plod from air-conditioned cradle to air-conditioned hearse.

THE DROUGHT HAS ENDED

Over the past several years
Summer rain has been a rare occurrence.
Fields were dampened with farmers' tears;
Dry summers a test of their endurance.

This year that problem has been solved.
A day without rain is a rare day indeed.
Has our weather simply evolved?
Or has some deeper force caused our sky to bleed?

Buttered toast falls buttered side down.
The great laws of nature are immutable.
All those things that cause us to frown
Are just Nature's notion of what's suitable.

To sole credit, I make no pretense
For this rain that's answered our farmers' prayers.
But it can't be just coincidence
That my roof's been off a month for repairs.

SUMMER'S DRIPPING DECADENCE

The August poem is short and sweet.
Even in this awful heat
Chocolate candy just can't be beat.

ARE YOU SURE IT'S SEPTEMBER?

Where has all of my summer gone?
From Memorial Day to Labor Day
It seemed more sprint than marathon.
Didn't this summer start just yesterday?

LABOR DAY BLUES

Is it possible that it's been
Three whole months since Memorial Day?
That summertime has gone again?
Look out kids! School is on its way.

CULTURE

BECOMING AMERICAN

GENERATION I

Hans, Juan, Izzy, and Sean
Came with nothing but willing hands
In hope of finding better lives.

Gert, Fe, Rachel, and Anne
Abandoned too their native lands,
Found good mates and became good wives.

Six days' hard work and sleep,
And one devoted to the Lord
Completed the immigrants' week.

Long hard hours would reap
Competent children headed toward
Great success; triumph of the meek.

BECOMING AMERICAN

GENERATION II

James, John, Betty, and Gail
Doctors, lawyers, and accountants
Filled ranks in this generation.

Not one of them would fail;
Much more modern than their parents,
Raised their offspring with love and patience.

BECOMING AMERICAN

GENERATION III

Lance, Kirk, Ashley, and Van
Grew up pampered and protected;
Chose freedom, not "superstitions."

Love for their fellow man,
And sex and pot they elected
As their "spiritual" missions.

Success was varied:
A movie producer, a rock star,
A rehab junkie, and a Madam.

Some have been married,
Each's fine house has a well-stocked bar,
Kids are a drag on those who've had 'em.

WE'VE CHANGED

We Americans have changed in our two hundred plus years.
I don't know whether that's good or bad, but I'm worried.
Today we're known for group handholding, hand wringing, and tears.
I don't know whether that's good or bad, but I'm worried.

The U.S. began with a lot of monumental men,
But monuments were raised slowly, and to just a few.
It took eighty-five years to get one for George Washington.
Now, not burning your draft card will get you a statue.
I don't know whether that's good or bad, but I'm worried.

In August 1813 the British burned Washington.
A year later we needed no healing ceremonies,
No searching introspection. The next year the war was won,
And life went on. We've become our forebears' antitheses.
I don't know whether that's good or bad, but I'm worried.

REDEFINING THE TEN SUGGESTIONS

I'll just bet that you thought that Moses got two tablets of stone.
Well, he didn't, you know, and you just need to correct that
   thought.
They were tablets of clay, a fact 'til now not gen'rally known,
And not firing the things allows some tweaking of what God
   wrought.

THE RELATIVE WEIGHT OF VIRTUES AND VICES

Our New Year's Resolutions are very brittle things,
Easily dropped and broken; all of them gone by spring.
With their demise unspoken, we to our habits cling,
'Cause virtues are a burden, and vices all have wings.

PEOPLE WATCHING AT THE MALL

The mirrored numbers of twelve and twenty-one
Bracket an interesting phase of a person's life.
Marked most notably by the phenomenon
Of defiance of convention, and attending strife.

Defiant nonconformity is the goal.
Bizarre piercings, black nails, dark makeup, and fright-wig hair
Mark persons playing the nonconformist role.
"Here we are, you'll have to get used to us," they declare.

And they all gather together at least once a day
To nonconform together, in a similar way.

ON THE ROAD TO THE BALKAN STATES OF AMERICA

Class warriors and race baiters are genuine folk heroes.
They claim they're doing good, and they do very well indeed.
If it weren't for the fiddling of these modern day Neros
Large groups of people wouldn't know they were victims in
    need.

They do very well, indeed, these champions of the "oppressed."
A house in the Hamptons and a condo in the City
Are minimum wage for those who know well how to protest.
Incidental societal damage is a pity.

Minor evil must be accepted for the greater good
A pity a double digit IQ comes to believe
That he's victimized, marginalized, or misunderstood,
And therefore feels the need to kill, and kill, and watch us
    grieve.

That his living standard is the envy of the whole world
Does not mean that this idiot has not been victimized.
He has; but not by America. His fate was unfurled
When mesmerized by the teachings of the self-canonized.

The man whose finger was on the trigger will surely die.
While all the men who pulled his strings will go on living high.

YOU CANNOT DEFAME THE DEAD

Admiral Sir Dexter Pitney-Land, KG, KB,
Was born at Exeter in the year seventeen three,
And died at Sal'sbury late in his 98th year.
His exemplary life had been lived devoid of fear.

A prodigy at seven, he performed before the Court,
Introducing the Queen to her first pianoforte.
And when he was eleven won first prize for *The Cohort*,
His epic poem tribute to one brave unit's foray.

Then at the age of eighteen, Oriel on him conferred
The Master of Arts Degree. 'Twas time to seek his fortune.
The choice seemed to be between Church and Bar, but Dexter heard
The call to Arms and the Sea, which call he answered quite soon.

The Fleet's oldest Midshipman was older by half than most.
But advancement was rapid for this remarkable man.
In 1721, he was on India's coast,
And stayed 'til that coast was rid of pirates and he, a hand.

In 1724 Dexter was a Lieutenant.
In 1729 he received his first Command.
Then, in only two years more, flew a Commodore's Pennant.
At the age of twenty-nine, he was Adm'ral Pitney-Land.

During the rest of his long life, he suppressed the trade in slaves,
Battled the French in the War of Austrian Succession,
At Abraham, heard drum and fife; saw Wolfe and Montcalm in
    graves,
Then he reached, as First Sea Lord, the peak of his profession.

Along the way, he married the daughter of a Viscount;
Was to her a good husband; gave her six girls and a son.
He wrote a commentary on the Sermon on the Mount;
Wrote music, poetry, and a book on navigation.

One sniv'ling Adm'ralty Clerk, feeling that he'd been slighted,
Found a man who said he'd been at Eton with the First Sea Lord
And claimed that late one cold night in a space dimly lighted,
Six boys had amused themselves, abusing themselves in a
    gourd.

The Clerk set loose the rumor, that Dexter was one of them;
And after the Adm'ral died, he published it as a fact.
A film is being made for mass market distribution
Dexter's life is advertised as "love and adventure packed."

It will be called RING OF FIRE, "the tale of a man in awe
In an age of repression, trying to straighten his head."
The homoerotic theme has its basis in the law:

NO ACTION WILL LIE FOR THE DEFAMATION OF THE
    DEAD!

SPECIAL DAYS

A DAY TO REMEMBER

The married life is a narrow course.
On either side are mines.
Birthdays, Anniversaries, and worse:
The dreaded Valentines.

My advice to the young man who seeks a wife,
Is to find himself a sweet young thing
Born on 14 FEB and stick with her for life.
And insist on a birthday wedding.

HAPPY DAY, VALENTINE!

Why do I love thee?
Let me count the whys:
You're sweet as can be,
And you make great fries!

You're the greatest of mothers,
To our humans and others;
And a very pretty person,
Whose life I'll never let worsen.

I love you because you're you!
I am your own clinging vine.
I know you'll always be true.
So, HAPPY DAY, VALENTINE!

THE FABULOUS FIRST

The first of the month
Is quite a day;
The best of the month
In ev'ry way.

Sorc'ry, magic, and
Wonders, the rule;
Frogs fly, dogs talk, and
It's April, fool!

IT'S YOUR DAY

Can you clean the vilest mess?
And love the person who made it?
Can you withstand a caress
Involving tears, dirt, snot, and spit?

You can; you have; it's your way.
You never look for another
To do the work of the day.
Why? Because you are a mother.

HAVE A HAPPY MOTHER'S DAY!

A NIGHT OF FRIGHT

A blinding flash, then a second, illuminate the night;
And thunder rolls from cloud to cloud across the darkened sky.
It's not a night to be abroad without a good bright light.
One never knows, on such a night, who or what might be nigh.

Then one by one the forms appear, obscure shadowy forms,
Gliding, floating upon the night, witches, ghouls, and monsters;
And ev'ry one is half your height; they're coming now in swarms.
They're ev'rywhere, these munchkin frights, these short, spectral trav'lers.

What sends these eerie figures forth into this night?
Does evil walk tonight, or do our eyes deceive?
Perhaps a calendar consult might shed some light.
October thirty-first, this night's All Hallows Eve.

CHILDREN AWAKENING TERRIFIED ON A COLD DECEMBER NIGHT

A scraping sound makes the heart pound.
A hush falls, and skin crawls, and all eyes lift.
A jingling ring, what is this thing?
Overhead? Filled with dread, we squirm and shift.

A peek outside. A shadow spied.
Down below. In the snow. It cannot be.
But spread below, upon the snow,
The shadow, on the snow, for all to see.

I see the roof. I see the roof.
But also, in the shadow, I see a sleigh.
And on the snow, I see also,
A teamster, and eight deer, lift up and away.

AN AMERICAN CHRISTMAS

'Tis the season to be jolly;
Spend our cash on ev'ry folly.
Not exactly in the spirit
Of the first, or even near it.
But don't be quick with condemnation—
'Tis the business of the nation.

A VERY MERRY YEAR-END FESTIVITIES CYCLE TO ALL

Twenty eighty-four of the current era is drawing to a close
And the full directorate wishes to disclose
The end of year festivities that it is their pleasure to impose.

Candletime will commence on the nineteenth day of the twelfth month this year
And overlap with the stable, tree, and reindeer.
Candles may be requisitioned, but citizens must buy their own beer.

All stables and trees must be in place no later than the twenty-fourth.
On the twenty-fifth there will be reindeer and sleighs on snow in the north
And where required in the south, snow machines will precede their going forth.

The twenty-sixth we'll commence our most traditional celebration.
Because ancient superstitions had played no part in its foundation,
The year-end festival of Kwanzaa has required no adaptation.

PETS

OH, TANNENBAUM!

The kitten was about three months old
When her people brought a tree inside.
The weather outside was very cold;
And it was with a great deal of pride
She watched her humans work so very hard
To provide a substitute for the yard.

A BEAUTIFUL STRAY CAME OUR WAY

(No One Is Perfect)

We have a beautiful dog. Her name is Babe, and
She is most thoroughly modern in every way.
Like the girl from Ipanema, she is tall and tan.
Gladly she loves and honors, but she will not obey!

A SUNNY MORNING ON THE LIVING ROOM CARPET

The dog and the cat lie sound asleep,
Nose to nose in a bright shaft of light.
Tiny specks of dust swirl, dance, and leap
To the rhythm of their breathing slight.

This house was the cat's from birth to four.
And then, one dark day, life filled with grief.
A great clumsy beast came through the door,
A big, ugly dog, who would not leave.

The humans brought it; seemed to like it.
She didn't know why, or how they could.
This dog lacked respect. Who could like it?
She ignored the cat; mocked her cathood!

Ev'ry time the dog would lumber past,
The cat would slap her, and be ignored.
A tail in the face, the parting blast,
And, in disbelief, her anger soared.

But then over time, life settled in
To a slow routine; and day by day,
Little by little, tol'rance set in.
She was a sister, not just a stray.

The dog and the cat lie sound asleep,
Nose to nose in a bright shaft of light.
Tiny specks of dust swirl, dance, and leap
To the rhythm of their breathing slight.

MONKEY GRASS REST STOP

My doggy loves that monkey grass;
It's her favorite p-mail drop.
In little clumps or waving mass,
A mandatory lift tail stop.

Now it's not the only place she sprinkles, you see,
But its leaves fill her face with crinkles,
'Cause it tickles her teats while she tinkles, tee hee;
It tickles her teats while she tinkles.

POLITICS

THE WAY WE CHOOSE OUR LEADERS

Charlie said that he would not decide
'Til he'd seen and heard each candidate.
Seeing and hearing them would provide
Just what he would need to separate
One from another and make his choice;
He votes for the man, not the party.
When he casts his vote we hear his voice.
We heard that voice loud, strong, and hearty.
The best P.R. machine was his choice.

George took the time to read the platforms,
Chose the one which best expressed his views,
Voted for that party which conforms
To those views; then waited for good news.
Charlie and George agree on most things;
Their opinions, very much the same;
But their votes fell on opposite wings,
And effective P.R. won the game.
Charlie's candidate got the brass rings.

George was disappointed by the vote,
But the next four years were just what he expected.
Charlie was elated by the vote,
But what came next left him completely dejected.

Charlie is now disillusioned with politics.
He says, "THEY are all the same: Lie, Cheat. Steal and Fix."

EXERCISING THE VOTE

Ours is not a Government of men.
Ours is a Government of laws.
Do you know who makes those laws, my friend?
The Party in power, because
It is the Party in power which has enough votes
To cram legislation down the opposition's throats.

Keep that in mind when you go to the polls.
Forget the man. Vote Party for your goals.

AMBITION

Ambition can be a wonderful thing when it is properly directed.
It can build railroads, and ships, and bridges. It can improve the lives of us all.
Driving progress, it can be the mainspring, delivering more than expected.
It can cure disease; build a heritage. It can improve the lives of us all.
Ambition can be a wonderful thing when it is properly directed.

When a man wants more for his family than he had when he was growing up,
And he studies hard and he works harder, that's ambition headed tow'rd success.
When that man builds up a bus'ness and he provides work for others climbing up,
His ambition is like a bread starter: growing, raising ev'ryone's success.
Ambition can be a wonderful thing when it is properly directed.

From the discovery of fire and the wheel to the very latest vaccine,
Ambition has been a major factor in the betterment of mankind's lot.
Ambition well directed is ideal; coupled with competence, a machine;
A machine that is man's benefactor in his efforts to improve his lot.
Ambition can be a wonderful thing when it is properly directed.

But what shall we say of raw ambition with no grounding in ability?
Someone might seek out a leadership role for the prestige rather than to serve.
Beware the man hunting for a mission to mask his lack of ability,
A parade to lead or a nice loophole through which to dance the Sidestep And Swerve.
Ambition can be a terrible thing when it's improperly directed.

WAR AND PEACE

THE LEARNING EXPERIENCE

When ev'rything seems to go wrong
We are tempted to despair.
But adversity makes us strong;
Helps us better to prepare.

... AND ON EARTH, PEACE TO MEN OF GOOD WILL

A deep, low rumble, as much felt as heard,
Rolled rapidly across the desert plain,
Climbed the hills, and smashed into the mountains,
Echoing among the high, snow wrapped peaks.

All men's eyes transfixed, not one spoke a word.
Blinding lights flashed in clouds of dust, not rain.
This sound and light was not God's work, but men's.
These Holy Days are filled with warriors' shrieks.

Perhaps next year will be the year of peace;
Perhaps there will be more men of good will;
But if there cannot be found more of these,
At least there'll be fewer whose will is ill.

CELEBRATION

Click, click, clickety-click, clicks,
Sounds of rims beaten by sticks;
Slap, it's a slap, and slap, and slap,
Shoes strike pavement, and people clap.

Clip-clop, clippety-clop, clop,
War horses strut, prance, and hop;
Steadier gaits followed by creaks
Mark the artill'ry. No one speaks.

Then drums thunder and fifes squeal,
People cheer and church bells peel.
Philadelphia's ours again.
The end's in doubt, but we can win.

Our spirits are high
'Though winds of war still vacillate,
This Fourth of July
In seventeen seventy-eight.

A JULY NIGHT ON FREEDOM'S TRAIL

Pop-poppity-pop; pop-pop, pop-pop.
Fi—izzz, swoosh; silence, whump!
Pop-pop-pop and whoosh; whump, whump, pop, pop!
Oohs and ahhs; children jump.

Yellows, blues, greens, reds; long streaks of light
Mar the black. What a sight!
Lights, shapes and starbursts defy the night.
Not the Fourth. A firefight.

THE SEA

WHY WE GO DOWN TO THE SEA IN SHIPS

On a cold winter's ev'ning
While he's sitting by the fire,
A seaman's mind gets something
Closely akin to desire.

It's a longing for the sea;
For balmy tropical nights,
With following wind and sea,
When the stars are brilliant lights.
When a soft breeze wraps around you,
And mere words cannot express
The effect it has upon you.
It's a lover's soft caress.

These are the things remembered
When you're safe and sound ashore;
No thoughts of storms unnumbered,
Rolls, thirty degrees and more.

Thus God provides for our nation's trade;
Thus he provides our ships with seamen.
For if our mem'ries he'd not degrade,
We'd know that the sea is a daemon.

STEAMING INTO THE WIND

When the gale is blowing on you and your hair is plastered back
When your nose is tryin' hard but your lungs can feel the lack,
When your eyes are burnin' red
And there's a lightness in your head:

You can scream and you can yell,
You can raise unholy hell;
You can curse and you can spit,
You can have a bloody fit;
You can call upon God's angels,
And the fallen ones as well;

But no matter how you cuss,
Or how awful is your fit,
It's only wasted fuss,
For that Damnable Wind WON'T QUIT!

THE SHALLOWS

They call them the shallows, these Indies waters;
And hotter than hell they are.
From the Celebes to Singapore, the bottom's never far.

The Dutch came seeking for Pearls and spice
In ships of wood and tar.
And many's the ship whose hull was ripped
On that bottom that's never far.

Now the Dutch are gone, the ships are steel,
And oil is the shining star.
But the waters don't change;
Treach'rous they are,
Looking for victims still.

If you venture out here, and you're going far,
Have for a shipmate, skill!

THIS AND THAT

WE MUST ALL HUMOR ONE ANOTHER

When a person gets to thinkin'
About the way the world goes round,
If that person gets to drinkin'
While he's thinkin', he'll think he's found
The secrets of the universe,
But which he won't have done, of course.

HI, I'M FROM THE GOV'MENT AND I'M HERE TO HELP

My government wants the best for me.
They've decreed a new, improved TV:
Digital and high definition,
A benevolent imposition.

So what if my eyesight's not 20/20?
Or if I watch with a little Chianti?
Or that the screen is small and far away?
We need this new standard without delay.

For those whose eyesight is 20/20,
Watch their TV without the Chianti,
And can afford a really big screen,
Their pictures will be the best ever seen.

My old TV will before long just die.
Of course there's a converter I can buy;
And I will likely buy some others too
For poor folks, when my income tax falls due.

My government surely wants the best for me;
They've even decreed a new, improved TV.
It's digital and it's high definition;
A truly benevolent imposition.

ODE TO THE FALLEN

When one has become comfortable with the notion
That something cannot be done,
It's just wearisome watching the dull build emotion
For a cause that can't be won.

And when that effort with success has been rewarded,
It's so very hard to find in one's heart—
To find in one's heart, forgiveness for the retarded;
And admit he might even have been smart.

STARTING OVER

It's hard to believe it's over;
I was just getting used to it.
I think I probably blew it.
At any rate, now it's over.

Next time I'm sure I'll do better.
I'm really going to try.
2003 has just flown by.
2004 will be better.

THE LILT OF IRISH MUSIC

Now, once upon a time, in a lush green Irish vale,
A young man in his prime languished in an English gaol.
The young man's name was Dan, and everyone knew his name;
Not for a rebel's plan, it was music made his fame.

His music could melt the heart of a stone,
And his voice filled the angels with envy.
A new tenant sat on the Viceroy's throne;
And fancied himself a musician, he.

Lord and Lady Plushbottom, from London fresh arrived,
Sought some immortality, and music seemed a gate.
They offered Dan his freedom; his spirits quick revived.
He said he'd immortalize their most outstanding trait.

And now you know the truth—truth stark, unvarnished, and bare,
Of just how Danny Boy gave us London Derriere

A SLIGHTLY HEAVIER OUNCE OF PREVENTION

(Or What You Get When You Take Preventative Measures)

Security is very high style,
And preventive measures busy the nation.
"Pop" semantics go that extra mile,
And add a syllable. Wow! PREVENTATION!

IT AIN'T NECESSARILY SO!

Perhaps influenced by the global warming enthusiasts,
Most folks are certain that we can control our environment;
But once in a while nature releases a couple of blasts
To remind us that, to our surprise and our astonishment,
Guess what? It ain't necessarily so!
Oh no, it ain't necessarily so.

LIVING IN INTERESTING TIMES

In the fifties while in high school and college,
I learned about hist'ry's major upheavals.
Tales of excitement expanded my knowledge:
Revolutions, warfare, blessings, and evils;
Disasters, floods, and pestilence cutting swathes
Across history's vast tableau; Mongols, Goths,
Saracens and Sioux, made for a heady brew
Of adventure, excitement, and derring-do.

Compared with the excitement of times gone by
Our era seemed to be exceedingly dull.
No major war, revolution, battle cry,
Or bomb throwers; we seemed to live in a lull.
"Boring," it seemed, was the watchword of our age.
But that has changed; now we're on another page.

To those who live it, any age is a fetter,
But between exciting and dull, dull is better.

THE ANATOMY OF HAIKU

You're five the first time;
Then seven, then five, no rhyme.
Haiku! Don't like you.

THE LANGUAGE LIVES, BUT IT'S AILING

I wish that I would never see an n. as active as a v.;
But verbs are being crowded out, and nouns are what it's all about.
I gift to you, you gift to me, dialogue-ing around the tree;
And then we'll conference about how nouns are in and verbs are out.

BIRTHDAYS

FOR MY FRESHEST GRANDCHILD

Welcome to our world, Miss Ayencie.
I think you'll find it to your liking.
It's a wond'rous world, just wait and see.
You'll find that life can be exciting.

The world has a lot to offer you,
And the world's improved because of you.

ONE YEAR OLD

Being one
Is lots of fun.

TWO YEARS OLD

No more one,
But life's still fun!

You'll soon be two.
Can you buckle your shoe?

Before you know it, three will be here.
And so it goes, year after year.

Four is great and five is greater.
Life gets better as time gets later.

From six through twenty-five it's time to learn.
From twenty-five on, it's time to earn.

Finally, you'll decide what you want to be.
And you'll be glad that you got that Ph.D.

THREE YEARS OLD

I think that three
Is a nice age to be.

Better than two,
It's a fine age for you.

From here to four
You'll always have more
Of all those things
Which the age of three brings.

Your job now is just to grow.
That is how life works, you know.

FOUR YEARS OLD

Well, well, it's time for four.
How could any person ask for more?
Three was nice, but a bit of a bore.
I think it's time for four.

I'll be so big when I am four.
When we have tea I'll be able to pour.
Just thinking about it makes my heart soar.
I'll be so big when I am four.

It is time now for four.
I'm feeling it to my very core;
I just don't care to wait anymore.
I know it's time for four!

FIVE YEARS OLD

A person can derive
A lot from being five,
Like starting to discern
That there's a lot to learn.

That's just the reason I've
Decided to be five.

SIX YEARS OLD

At one, one's hardly done.
At two, you've not a clue.
At three, you start to be.
At four, you learn lots more.
At five, you are alive.
But SIX is LOTS OF KICKS!

SEVEN YEARS OLD

When a person is seven, it's almost heaven.
She's old enough for reading; that's good mind seeding.
Now our girl has reached that age; she'll soon be a sage.
It won't last too long. In a flash the year'll be gone.
And you will say then, oh to be seven again!

EIGHT YEARS OLD

I am told that you are eight.
Now how can that be true?

If you keep on at this rate,
There'll be no little you!

NINE YEARS OLD

What a day!
Right here in May!

Make a wish,
Blow the candles.
Fill your dish,
Kick your sandals!

Being nine
Is really fine.

TEN YEARS OLD

You're halfway to twenty;
But for now, ten's plenty.

ELEVEN YEARS OLD

She's eleven now, and growing fast;
I'm wondering how that time has passed.
Only yesterday I carried her.
In my arms she lay as if she were
Content just to stay right there in her
Infancy and our soft, loving care.
But something's gone sour. How could she dare
To grow up like that? Without warning?
To grow up like that? Without warning!

TWELVE YEARS OLD

Twelve is a very good age.
It's an age that sets the stage
For the most difficult age.
Your teens are on the next page.

THIRTEEN YEARS OLD

Our little girl has become a teen:
An event that I hadn't foreseen.

I suppose that it had to happen;
But I just didn't expect it so soon.
Why can't we just start over again,
And all of us age as in Brigadoon?

Printed in the United States
58884LVS00002B/22-72